Meet Me at Luigi's

LILLENAS DRAMA

Meet Me at Luigi's

An Interactive Dinner Theatre Event in Six Scenes

by Tom and Celesta Letchworth

KANSAS CITY, MO 64141

Meet Me at Luigi's
Copyright © 1998 by Tom and Celesta Letchworth. All rights reserved.

Print rights administered by Lillenas Publishing Co.

No part of this publication may be reproduced, stored in retrieval system, or transmitted, in any form or by any means, electronic, mechanical, photocopying, recording, or otherwise, without the prior permission of the copyright administrator.

This is a royalty play. Permission to perform these works is granted when a Production Pack containing scripts for the cast and director is purchased and the royalty is paid two weeks prior to the performance(s). The performance licensing fee for each of these plays is $30.00 for the first performance and $20.00 for each subsequent performance. Please use the form in the back of this book to register your performance(s) and to submit the royalty payment. You may make copies of the form or submit the information in the form of a letter.

The following should appear in your printed program:
"Produced by special arrangement with Lillenas Publishing Co."

Lillenas Publishing Company
P.O. Box 419527
Kansas City, MO 64141
Phone: 816-931-1900 • Fax: 816-753-4071
E-mail: drama@lillenas.com

Printed in the United States.
Cover design by Marie Tabler

Acknowledgments

Thanks to my dramatic guinea pigs—the teens of Salem United Methodist Church—who originally produced *Meet Me at Luigi's*. They endured many long rehearsals and my repeated attempts to teach them how to talk in a "Philly" accent.

Special thanks goes to a terrific role model and mentor for Salem's young people—Tom Frase. That's why he was cast as the very first Gino. It's easy to create characters and write dialogue when you can imagine such a fine cast performing it.

We also appreciate our audiences who came from all over the central Arkansas area—it's a lot easier to perform for sell-out crowds.

And we will always be grateful to Paul Miller—more than an editor. He served as our pastor and our encourager.

Lastly, in the tradition of Luigi, we want to thank our own Mommas, Billie Nell and Celesta Rose. They loved us. All the time.

Dedication

With very special thanks to God,

who is still in the business of

creating comets and healing broken relationships.

Contents

Synopsis 11

Cast of Characters 13

Scene Description and Prop List 15

Performance Suggestions 17

Pronunciation Guide 19

Scene 1: "Bubba, Bubba, Who's Got the Bubba?" 21

Scene 2: "When Does a Car Have Five Tires?" 27

Scene 3: "I Dream of Bubba and His Lock of Hair" 31

Scene 4: "But My Stomach Doesn't Speak Italian" 40

Scene 5: "Apocalypse, *Now?!*" 49

Scene 6: "Whatza Matter for You, Eh?" 55

Synopsis

Here's a great way to dress up those church spaghetti fundraisers. Transform your church's fellowship hall into Luigi's Italian Restaurant, where the audience eats an Italian meal, periodically interrupted by six scenes of a one-act comedy. (Lasagna, veal parmigiana, and other Italian main courses work just as well as spaghetti.)

The concept is a "you are there" dinner theatre experience. The actors utilize the entire fellowship hall as the stage. That means the audience is part of the show. We can't have the play take place at Luigi's Restaurant and not have customers, now can we? Audiences love to be part of the whole *experience,* as the actors stay in character between scenes, serving the food.

Luigi's is packed with tourists and news media people who have come to observe a comet in this one of only 23 towns in America with an 80 percent visibility of this astronomical phenomenon.

Gino, co-owner and manager of Luigi's, and his brother Luigi, the head chef and a man of few words (actually five), implore the local teenagers to help serve dinner to all these customers (the audience).

During the evening's events, Albert, the school brain, is only too eager to offer information about the comet, and Jonathan, the philosopher of the group, voices his own reflections about the human condition. Dave and Rusty wash dishes and clear tables while they're not tripping and spilling food. Betsy tries to cut a lock of Bubba's hair to put under her pillow during the comet so he'll fall in love with her, but she discovers that acquiring a lock of hair isn't as easy as it sounds. Bubba has his own set of problems, though. As the son of Luigi, he's the head waiter, but he needs to get off work early for reasons he dare not tell his Uncle Gino.

The cast also includes Jerry, the school football hero, and his cheerleader girlfriend, Buffy; Gloria, Betsy's nerdy friend; Colleen and Darlene, sticking together like snobby birds of a feather; Maryanne, the new waitress; Maria, the flaky waitress; and local teens Steve and Nancy.

The play is divided into six scenes. The audience eats between scenes. After scene one, the actors serve the beverages and bread. After scene two, the salad. After scene three, the spaghetti. After scene four, the dessert. After scene five, refill beverages.

Gino says, "Come. You will sit. You will eat. You will cry a little. You will laugh a lot. And only can you do this at Luigi's."

So how about it? Will you meet me at Luigi's?

Cast of Characters

GINO: *Manager and co-owner of Luigi's. He is Luigi's brother. Very friendly, relates well to teenagers. Gino talks with his hands.*

MARIA: *Flaky waitress. She is Luigi's daughter, which also makes her Bubba's sister and Gino's niece.*

MARYANNE: *New waitress. Maryanne is a normal teenager.*

LUIGI: *Cook and co-owner of Luigi's. He is Gino's brother and Maria and Bubba's father. He mostly stays in the kitchen, cooking and grumbling. He's a man of few words. Actually, five words. This role is perfect for a youth counselor who can keep the actors quiet in the "kitchen." He doesn't have to worry about his entrance cues. Each time he is to enter, someone yells, "Yo, Luigi." If Luigi misses the cue, the other actor can just repeat himself until Luigi comes out of the kitchen. He has actual lines in Scene 6, providing the climax of the play. Although few, these lines and stage directions are very important and must be worked with Gino and Bubba until they are fine-tuned.*

JERRY: *Football player.*

BUFFY: *Cheerleader.*

COLLEEN: *Snooty teenager.*

DARLEEN: *Colleen's equally snooty sidekick. Her lines and actions are exact mimics of Colleen.*

JONATHAN: *The philosopher of the group.*

DAVE: *Clumsy busboy. (See suggestions on the next page for combining the two busboys.)*

RUSTY: *Clumsy busboy.*

Steve: *An average teenager, if there is such a thing.* (See suggestions below for combining Steve and Nancy's lines, or dividing them among the cast or extras.)

Nancy: (See Steve.)

Albert: *The nerdy science lover of the group.*

Betsy: *Boy-crazy teenager, but also popular and well-liked.*

Gloria: *Very nerdy teenager. The only volume her voice knows is "loud."*

Bubba: *Luigi's son. Bubba is the quintessential "angry young man."*

Flexibility in the size of the cast was our main priority when writing *Meet Me at Luigi's*. The script, as is, can be performed by 15 teens and 2 adults. With a few changes, the script can accommodate as few as 12 teens and 2 adults or as many as 53 teens and no adults. Here are some suggested changes:

Steve and Nancy's lines can be played by one actor, or you may divide them up for as many as 38 actors. If there is a shortage of actors, you may delete these characters and distribute their lines among the other characters.

A few changes may be necessary if Steve and Nancy's lines are delivered by one actor. For example, delete lead-in lines like "Oh, yeah" (Steve, middle of Scene 1) and, "Yo, Bubba" (Nancy, beginning of Scene 2).

Dave and Rusty can be played by one person. In that case, change Rusty's line when he enters in Scene 1 to: "Yo, Gino! You called? *(He sees Marianne again.)* Oh. Hi, again. *(He trips and falls.)*" Then change Gino's line immediately following that to: "Make that two waitresses and a LOVESICK clumsy busboy!"

The two adult roles can be played by teens acting as adults. We suggest you do this as a last resort. The two adults add some stability to the rehearsals, and the role of Gino is that of a mentor, best played by someone the teens can respect as counselor and friend off the stage.

Gino can be played by a female. Her name's "Gina," and she is Luigi's sister.

Scene Description and Prop List

The entire fellowship hall is Luigi's Restaurant. It can be an elegant Italian restaurant, but more than likely it is a low-budget downtown hangout. Plastic flowers in vases or bottles at each table, red and white checkered tablecloths, and fish nets draped on the wall with Christmas tree lights will help create that ambiance.

Frame the first dollar Luigi and Gino earned and hang it next to Mama's picture. Mama's picture works best if it is as large as you can get. We took pictures of "Mama" with black and white film, and asked our developer to print it as a brown-on-brown "old" photograph. Then we blew it up to poster size and "framed" it by nailing wood trim around it.

Tables for cast members can be placed at the front of the fellowship hall, or they can be interspersed within the audience if the room is small. If it is possible to elevate these tables on blocks, they will be more visible for the audience. Putting these tables on a stage will make it more difficult for the audience to feel like part of the experience, but it still can work.

At least three tables are needed. One for Buffy and Jerry and friends, one for Gino to use when counseling Bubba, and one for Colleen and Darlene to retreat to. The first two tables need to be visible for the entire audience, since the actors will deliver lines while sitting there. Colleen and Darlene's table can be anywhere.

The table Gino uses when he counsels Bubba should have two chairs. Gino will pull out the chairs and turn them sideways, so they face each other, when he counsels Bubba in *Scene 2*, and when he counsels Bubba and Luigi in *Scene 6*.

A table should be set up as a "beverage station." This is where you'll keep water pitchers and ice. Rusty and Dave bump into this table.

Scene 1
Saltshakers (Maria)
Tray (Gino)
Aprons (at least for Dave and Luigi)
Tray with two pitchers (Dave)
Tray of silverware (Rusty)

Scene 2
Two salads (Make these salads "lettuce-only," so they won't stain the customer's clothes.) (Rusty)

Scene 3
Scissors (Betsy)
Phone (This is optional. Gloria can go offstage to use the "phone.")
Napkin or towel (Gino)

Scene 4
Watch (Albert)
Plastic flower in a vase, preferably on a customers' table (Gino and Jonathan)

Scene 5
Bouquet of plastic flowers in a vase, preferably on a different customers' table (Betsy)

Scene 6
Plastic bag with hair in it (Betsy)
Coatrack or hook to hang apron on (Luigi)

Performance Suggestions

Use music to set the atmosphere as your guests arrive and as interlude music in between scenes while the guests are eating. We suggest Italian music, opera music, anything with Luciano Pavarotti or Placido Domingo singing, or accordion music. Better yet, use a strolling musician who plays mandolin, accordion, or violin. Or ask some members of the church choir to sing selections from Italian operas.

Blocking can be tricky with a large cast. Designate two or three "away places" where the actors can go and hang out when they aren't involved in the dialogue. The beverage station works well as an away place, as does a doorway or a soda machine.

Make sure the actors stay in character between scenes while they serve the audience. This is a good acting exercise for the cast, and it makes the evening more fun for the audience.

Lasagna is mentioned in the script as the main dish. Change these lines accordingly if you're serving something else.

Warn the audience about the interrupted schedule for dinner by printing the courses in the program with the scene titles:

Scene 1: "Bubba, Bubba, Who's Got the Bubba?"
   Beverage and Bread

Scene 2: "When Does a Car Have Five Tires"
   Salad

Scene 3: "I Dream of Bubba and His Lock of Hair"
   Luigi's Lasagna

Scene 4: "But My Stomach Doesn't Speak Italian"
   Dessert

Scene 5: "Apocalypse, *Now?!*"
   Refill Beverages

Scene 6: "Whatza Matter for You, Eh?"

Pronunciation Guide

When using this guide, pronounce "oh" with a long *o* sound, and pronounce "ah" like a doctor, "Open your mouth and say ah."

Luigi (loo-WEE-jee)
Maria (mah-REE-yah)
Mama mia (MAH-mah MEE-yah)
Bubba (BUH-bah)
Ey (long *a* sound)
Eh (this is a nasal sounding *a*, as in "an")
Gino (JEE-no)
Ciao (Chow, as in the dog food)
Capisce (cah-PEESH)
Aiii (sounds like the word "eye"; draw it out to almost two syllables)
Correctomundo (cor-rect-oh-MOON-doh)
Kemosabee (kee-moh-SAH-bee)
Exactamundo (egg-zak-tah-MOON-doh)
Mach schnell (mawk shnell)
Che sara, sara (kay sah-RAH sah-RAH)
Carmine (sounds like a compound word made up of "car" and "mine"; put the accent on "car")
Gauche (gosh, with a long *o* sound.)
Domenic Pizarro (DOH-meh-nick pee-ZAH-roh)
Potiphar (POT-ih-far)
Jasmine (JAZZ-min)
Luciano Vincent Anthony DiDonato (loo-chee-AH-noh VIN-cent ANN-toh-nee dee-doh-NAH-toh)
Coma (COH-mah)
Rosa (ROH-sah)

El Grande (sounds like the letter *l* GRAHN-day)
Bueno (BWAY-noh)
Lucia . . . (loo-chee-AH. This is on the last page, when Luigi starts to say "Luciano" but corrects himself.)

MEET ME AT LUIGI'S

Scene 1
"Bubba, Bubba, Who's Got the Bubba?"

(MARIA *is filling saltshakers as* GINO *and* MARYANNE *enter from kitchen.*)

GINO *(speaking over his shoulder to* MARYANNE, *so he does not notice the audience)*: And that's the end of the grand tour of Luigi's. *(Turns his back to audience)* Maria! Meet our new waitress, Maryanne.

MARIA: Hi.

MARYANNE: Hi.

GINO: Maria! Good for you! You finished the saltshakers already! *(He takes a tray.)* Here. I'll get the pepper shakers off the tables for you. *(He turns toward audience's tables.)* MAMA MIA! *(He drops tray.)* Where did all these people come from?

MARIA: Uhmm. A bus?

GINO: How long have they been sitting there?

MARIA: Uhmm. A while?

GINO: Why don't they have any drinks?

MARIA: Uhmm. I don't know, why?

GINO: OK. Let's go over this one more time. You are a waitress, Maria. When a customer comes in and sits down at a table, the waitress—that's you—asks the customer what he or she would like to drink. Do you think you can do that?

MARIA: By myself?

GINO: Maryanne will help you. And Bubba should be here. Where IS Bubba?

MARIA: Bubba?

GINO: Your brother, Bubba.

MARIA: Oh yeah. Bubba.

GINO: Yes. Where is he?

(JERRY, BUFFY, COLLEEN, *and* DARLENE *enter.*)

JERRY: Yo, Luigi!

LUIGI *(enters from kitchen):* Ey!

JERRY: Got any fresh garlic bread?

LUIGI: Whatza matter for you, eh? *(He exits to kitchen.)*

GINO *(greets* JERRY *with a high five):* Yo, Jerry! How did football practice go today? Ready for the big game?

JERRY: Better be. Coach called off practice today on account of the comet. *(He sits at a table.)*

BUFFY *(following* JERRY *to table):* Yeah, Mrs. Wilson called off cheerleading practice too. *(She sits.)*

COLLEEN *(sashays across room to another table):* All because of a stupid comet.

DARLENE *(following* COLLEEN's *every move):* Yeah. All because of a stupid comet. (COLLEEN *and* DARLENE *sit.)*

MARYANNE: That must be why all these people are here.

GINO: Mama mia! I almost forgot! Maria—tell Luigi we got customers already. *(He starts to put saltshakers on the audience's tables.)*

MARIA *(does not move)*: OK.

GINO: Maria!

MARIA: Yeah?

GINO: I asked you to tell Luigi we got a room full of customers!

MARIA: I know.

GINO: Then why don't you tell him?

MARIA: Oh. Did you mean now?

GINO: NOW!

MARIA: All right. You don't have to shout, you know. *(She yells.)* Yo, Papa!

LUIGI *(enters from kitchen)*: Ey!

MARIA: Uhmm.

MARYANNE *(prompting MARIA)*: We have a room full of customers.

MARIA: Oh yeah. We have a room full of customers!

LUIGI: Whatza matter for you, eh? *(He exits to kitchen.)*

GINO: We need Bubba. WHERE is Bubba?

(JONATHAN, STEVE, NANCY, and DAVE enter.)

DAVE *(running past the others, he makes a beeline to the aprons)*: Yo, Luigi!

LUIGI *(enters from kitchen)*: EY!

DAVE *(tying apron on)*: Sorry I'm late. *(He runs over to the beverage station and grabs a tray with two pitchers.)*

JONATHAN: Yeah man, the traffic is incredible at the courthouse.

DAVE: I'll fill these with ice water right away. *(He notices MARYANNE on his way to the kitchen.)* Oh, hi. *(He walks toward MARYANNE.)* My name is . . . *(he trips and drops the pitchers)* Dave.

LUIGI: Whatza matter for you, eh? *(He exits to kitchen.)*

DAVE *(picks up tray and pitchers)*: I'm sorry.

GINO *(takes tray and pitchers from DAVE)*: Hey, Dave. At least this time they're empty, eh? Go on, now. Luigi's got some pans for you to wash.

(DAVE exits to kitchen.)

JONATHAN *(looks at audience)*: Wow. Looks like you've got mega customers, Gino.

GINO: And only two waitresses and a clumsy busboy.

RUSTY *(enters from kitchen)*: Yo, Gino! You called?

GINO: Make that TWO clumsy busboys!

RUSTY: Where?

GINO *(to Mama's picture)*: Mama. I know you said life is NOT a bowl of cherries. But what am I gonna do with all this fruitcake? *(To RUSTY)* Ask Luigi how much longer for the salads.

RUSTY: Sure thing, boss. *(He stumbles elaborately into the beverage table on his way back to the kitchen.)*

STEVE: Where's Bubba?

GINO: That's the question I've been asking for the last 30 minutes. Where is Bubba?

NANCY: Maybe he's down at the courthouse. *(She moves to an "away place.")*

STEVE *(following NANCY)*: Oh yeah. Those scientists are setting up a telescope in the vacant lot across from the courthouse.

JONATHAN *(strolling as he philosophizes)*: That's an interesting term: vacant lot. It's not really vacant. There's plenty of dirt, trash, broken bottles. But it's called a "vacant" lot because there's no building. We're a society that defines itself by buildings. Four walls and a roof. *(He turns, dramatically, and points.)* That should tell us something about the human condition.

(BETSY, ALBERT, and GLORIA enter, single file.)

BETSY: Yo, Luigi!

LUIGI *(enters from kitchen)*: EY!

BETSY: Are you ready for the comet?

LUIGI: Whatza matter for you, eh? *(He exits to kitchen.)*

GLORIA: Betsy, that's so stupid. How do you get READY for a comet?

ALBERT *(stops dead in his tracks and turns around.* GLORIA *nearly runs into him)*: Actually, Gloria, societies have been able to prepare for comets for centuries. The comet was one of the first astronomical phenomena that could be anticipated through scientific calculations.

COLLEEN *(walking toward* ALBERT, *teasing)*: Albert!

ALBERT *(obviously excited to speak with* COLLEEN): Yes, Colleen?

COLLEEN: Have you ever considered studying English as a second language?

DARLENE *(following close behind* COLLEEN): Yeah, have you ever considered studying English as a second language?

ALBERT: A SECOND language? Forgive me, but I'm not sure I understand.

COLLEEN *(turns to* DARLENE): See what I mean, Darlene?

(COLLEEN *and* DARLENE *laugh as they walk back to their table.)*

BETSY: Yo, Luigi!

LUIGI *(enters from kitchen)*: EY!

BETSY: Is Bubba in the kitchen?

LUIGI: Whatza matter for you, eh? *(He exits to kitchen.)*

MARYANNE: Bubba's not here yet.

GLORIA *(to* MARYANNE): Who are you?

GINO: Everybody, listen up! This is Maryanne, our new waitress. Now—has anyone seen Bubba?

BETSY: No. I thought he'd be here. I wanted to—uh—talk to him.

JERRY: Yo, Luigi!

LUIGI *(enters from kitchen):* EY!

JERRY: Where's that garlic bread I ordered?

LUIGI: Whatza matter for you, eh? *(He exits to kitchen.)*

GINO *(walking to* JERRY's *table):* Can't you see we're a little busy?

JERRY: Yeah, so?

GINO: Sooooooo. I'm short on help. Roll up your sleeves and get to work. All of you!

JERRY: Doing what?

GINO *(pulls back* JERRY's *chair, helping him to his feet):* You can start by serving the customers their drinks.

COLLEEN *(stands, indignantly):* You have GOT to be kidding.

DARLENE *(à la* COLLEEN*):* Yeah, you have GOT to be kidding.

BUFFY: Where did they all come from, anyway?

STEVE *(joining group):* I bet they're here to see the comet. The whole town is swarming with tourists.

ALBERT: Ironically, our little town is only one of 23 locations on our entire planet that is in a position of 80 percent visibility for the comet.

JERRY: Yeah, well that's not MY problem.

GINO: That's right, Jerry. *(He massages* JERRY's *shoulders.)* Your problem is— *(he playfully puts his hands around* JERRY's *neck)* what will Gino do with you if you don't get to work. NOW!

JERRY: All right, all right. *(He exits to kitchen, and the other teens, except* MARIA, *follow.)*

GINO *(to audience):* We are so happy you chose Luigi's for your dining pleasure this evening. Please, sit back, relax, and prepare yourselves for a sumptuous Italian meal.

RUSTY *(enters with a tray of silverware):* Yo, Gino! Here's the clean . . . *(he trips and drops the tray of silverware)* silverware. I'm sorry.

GINO: Allow me to introduce our head busboy, Rusty, who is on his way BACK to the kitchen to wash more SILVERWARE! *(Sweetly, to audience)* And now, we will serve you your drinks. Ciao!

MARIA: Uncle Gino?

GINO: Yes, Maria. What is it now?

MARIA: I was just wondering. Do you know where Bubba is?

GINO *(exits to kitchen):* Mama mia!

*(The actors serve the customers drinks and bread between **Scene 1** and **Scene 2**.)*

Scene 2
"When Does a Car Have Five Tires?"

(As the scene begins, STEVE and NANCY are hanging out; LUIGI and GINO are in the kitchen; BETSY, GLORIA, and MARIA are in an "away place"; COLLEEN and DARLENE are sitting at their table; JERRY and BUFFY are sitting at their table; and the rest of the cast can be either in the kitchen or an "away place." BUBBA is outside.)

(BUBBA enters.)

STEVE *(yells):* Yo, Luigi!

LUIGI *(enters from kitchen):* EY!

STEVE: Bubba's here!

LUIGI: Whatza matter for you, eh? *(He exits to kitchen.)*

BUBBA *(sarcastically):* Thanks a lot, Steve.

NANCY: Yo, Bubba. You ready for the comet?

BUBBA: Not exactly.

GINO *(enters from kitchen):* Bubba! Where have you been?

BUBBA: Out.

GINO: I see. Come—we'll talk. *(He takes* BUBBA *aside.)*

BUBBA: There's nothin' to talk about.

GINO: Yes, yes, I know. *(He walks to at an empty table and pulls out a chair, turning it sideways.)* Come—sit.

BUBBA *(sits at table but continues to avoid eye contact):* I told you, there's nothin' to talk about.

GINO *(pulls out the other chair, turning it sideways, and sits, facing* BUBBA*):* Bubba—look at me. (BUBBA *looks up.)* See? It's me—your old Uncle Gino. Since when do you have nothing to say to your Uncle Gino, eh?

BETSY *(approaches* BUBBA'S *table, with* GLORIA *close behind):* Hi, Bubba. Uhmm—I was just wondering, uh—are you going to be getting a haircut soon?

BUBBA: Who wants to know?

BETSY: Oh, I don't know. We were all just talking about haircuts, and your name came up in the conversation. *(She laughs nervously.)* How about that.

GLORIA: I don't remember talking about haircuts.

BETSY: Gloria! Don't you have something else to do?

JERRY: What's the deal with the hair?

BETSY: It's not against the law to ask somebody about their hair!

COLLEEN *(strolling past* BETSY *to other side of room):* In that case, who styles YOUR hair, Betsy—your mom?

DARLENE *(right behind* COLLEEN*):* Yeah, who styles YOUR hair, Betsy—your mom?

(COLLEEN *and* DARLENE *laugh as they walk to an "away place."*)

GINO: Yo, Luigi!

LUIGI *(enters from kitchen):* EY!

GINO: You need help making the salads?

LUIGI: Whatza matter for you, eh? *(He exits to kitchen.)*

GINO: Kids—you heard him. Go help Luigi with the salads.

STEVE: But he said—

GINO: I know what he SAID. And I know what he MEANT. Now go!

JERRY: Why do we have to make salads? I thought we just had to do drinks.

GINO: Because Gino says so. Capisce?

JERRY: Yeah, capisce.

(Everyone but MARIA *and* BUBBA *exits to kitchen.* MARIA *is still in an "away place" and* BUBBA *remains seated.)*

GINO *(to* BUBBA*):* So. You're 45 minutes late for work. Where were you?

MARIA *(walks quietly behind* GINO, *then speaks, startling* GINO*):* Uncle Gino?

GINO *(recovering):* What is it, Maria?

MARIA: Uhmm. I just thought you should know. Uhmm. Bubba's here.

GINO: Thank you, Maria, for this news bulletin flash.

MARIA: Sure.

GINO: And now you will help Luigi with the salads?

MARIA *(does not move):* Uhmm. Yeah.

GINO *(motions toward kitchen):* In the KITCHEN?

MARIA: Uhmm. Yeah. Sure. *(She exits to kitchen.)*

GINO: All right. I'm listening.

BUBBA: I had a flat tire.

GINO: That was your excuse yesterday.

BUBBA: So, I had ANOTHER flat tire, OK?

GINO *(gets up and paces):* You ALSO had a flat tire the day before yesterday and the day before that, AND the day before that. *(Turns to* BUBBA*)* Look at me, Bubba. This is your Uncle Gino you're talking to—not an idiot off the street. *(Walks to Mama's picture)* My dear, departed mother—your grandmother—scraped and saved every penny she could get her hands on so that I could go to college and become an accountant. And now you are insulting MY intelligence and the love and faith of my dead mother by thinking that I cannot count to five? FIVE tires, Bubba. Your car does not have FIVE TIRES!

BUBBA: OK, so I didn't have a flat.

GINO *(sits back down):* So talk to me, Bubba. Talk to me.

BUBBA *(he pauses in anguish):* I can't, Uncle Gino. You—you wouldn't understand.

RUSTY *(enters with a salad in each hand):* Yo, Gino. Salad's ready. You want us to serve them?

GINO: Yes, of course.

(RUSTY *approaches a customer's table.)*

GINO: Remember, Rusty—serve from the left—

RUSTY *(spills salad in customer's lap and/or floor):* Oops! Sorry.

GINO *(shaking head):* Aiii. Mama mia. And vacuum from the right. *(He exits to kitchen.)*

(The actors serve the customers' salad between **Scene 2** *and* **Scene 3**.*)*

Scene 3
"I Dream of Bubba and His Lock of Hair"

(DAVE *and* MARYANNE *are talking in one corner of the room.* LUIGI *and* GINO *are in the kitchen.* JERRY *and* BUFFY *are sitting at their table.* BUBBA *and* ALBERT *and the other teens are standing to the side, talking.* MARIA, BETSY, *and* GLORIA *are talking at the other side of the room. The scene begins as* BETSY *sneaks up behind* BUBBA *with a pair of scissors and unsuccessfully tries to cut a lock of hair off the back of his head.*)

BUBBA: OUCH! (BETSY *runs backward as he wheels around.*) Betsy! (*He walks toward her.*) What d'ya think you're doing?

BETSY *(hiding scissors behind her back):* Nothing. What makes you think I was doing anything?

BUBBA *(still rubbing back of his head):* What's that behind your back?

BETSY: MY back? Good question. (*She places the scissors on the table behind her.*) What's behind MY back? (*She waves both hands.*) Nothing! See? (*She laughs nervously.*) And nothing's up my sleeve, either.

MARIA *(hands* BETSY *the scissors):* Uhmm. Here's your scissors, Betsy. You left them on table number 4.

BETSY: Thanks a lot, Maria.

BUBBA: Scissors?

BETSY: It's not against the law to own a pair of scissors, you know!

JONATHAN *(strolling as he philosophizes):* Did you know that in some states, it's against the law to spit on the sidewalk? But it's perfectly legal for a pregnant woman to endanger the health of her unborn child by using tobacco and alcohol products. (*He turns, dramatically, and points.*) That should tell us something about the human condition.

GLORIA: Jonathan! You shouldn't talk about people being PREGNANT in a restaurant! That's so disgusting!

COLLEEN *(strolling past* GLORIA *to other side of room)*: Oh, you're so right, Gloria. Why, that rates right up there on the "disgusting" list with people who wear retainers!

DARLENE *(right behind* COLLEEN*)*: Yeah, people who wear retainers!

GLORIA: Are you talking about me? Because I hope you know that I only wear MY retainer at night!

COLLEEN *(stops and turns to* DARLENE*)*: See? I told you, Darlene!

(COLLEEN *and* DARLENE *laugh as they move to an "away place."* GLORIA *and* JONATHAN *move to a different "away place."* BETSY *sits at* JERRY *and* BUFFY's *table.)*

GINO *(enters from kitchen)*: Yo, Maria. Did everyone get a salad?

MARIA: Uhmm. Salad?

GINO: Salad. The green stuff we serve before dinner.

MARIA: Oh yeah. Salad.

GINO: So, did everybody get one?

MARIA: Uhmm. Get one what?

GINO: SALAD! Did everyone get a salad?!

MARIA: Oh. Uhmm. Yeah, I think so. *(She moves to an "away place.")*

GINO: Good. Listen, Bubba, I have to help Luigi with the lasagna. But as soon as it's done, we talk. Capisce? *(He exits to kitchen.)*

BUBBA: Yeah, capisce.

(STEVE *and* NANCY *approach* BUBBA.)

NANCY: Trouble?

BUBBA: He didn't buy my story about the flat tire.

STEVE: Bummer. So how'd you make out with the media?

BUBBA: Total wash-out. They're too busy interviewing those scientists about the comet.

STEVE: But you wrote that song about the comet. That should be your ticket in.

BUBBA: Sure, if I could ever get through to 'em.

JERRY: Yo, Bubba. You still goin' to dress rehearsal tonight?

BUBBA: Yeah.

(STEVE *and* NANCY *move back as* JERRY *and* BUFFY *approach.*)

JERRY *(gets up and puts hand on* BUBBA's *shoulder;* BUFFY *is right behind him):* You think you can give Buffy a ride? I need to go home and change first.

BUBBA: Sure.

BUFFY: I need to get there early, is that OK?

BUBBA: Yeah. I gotta do sound checks anyway.

BUFFY: Great! 'Cause we need a LOT of extra practice on our human pyramid! I'm on the very top, you know. I wasn't supposed to be, but Sara Littleton got sick with the flu, so—I'M IT! The top, I mean. Oh, Jerry—I am soooo nervous.

JERRY: Yeah, yeah. You'll be great, Babe.

BUFFY: I mean, there's a rumor going around that some TV news reporters might come to the talent show—you know—since they're here anyway for the comet?

BUBBA *(very interested):* Where'd you hear that?

BUFFY: From Monica Phillips.

BUBBA: How's she know?

BUFFY: Dave told her.

BUBBA: Yo, Dave!

(DAVE *continues talking to* MARYANNE.)

BUBBA: Da-VID!

DAVE: What?

BUBBA: Come here!

DAVE: Oh, man. *(He walks to* BUBBA.*)* This better be good. I was just about to ask Maryanne out.

BUBBA: Who's Maryanne?

DAVE: The new waitress your Uncle Gino hired. *(Pause)* I think she likes me.

NANCY: Yeah, right.

DAVE: Yeah, right!

NANCY: She's just being polite.

DAVE: Says you!

BUBBA *(interrupting fight):* Shut up, everybody! Dave—what's this about the media showing up at the talent show tonight?

DAVE: Yeah, how about that.

BUBBA: How do you know?

DAVE: Albert told me.

BUBBA: Albert!

ALBERT *(walks to* BUBBA*)*: At your service.

DAVE: Excuse me, but I have some very important business to take care of. *(He moves to* MARYANNE.*)*

BUBBA: Who told you the TV guys would be at the talent show?

ALBERT: They did.

BUBBA: They who?

ALBERT: The news correspondents.

BUBBA: You talked to the reporters?

ALBERT: You bet your beeper.

BUBBA: That's impossible. No one could get to them. I tried.

ALBERT: Actually, I didn't get to them. THEY approached ME.

STEVE: What would they want with you?

ALBERT: The mayor told them about my blue ribbon comet exhibit at the science fair.

COLLEEN *(walks to edge of those in conversation):* Yeah, right. I suppose CBS wants an EXCLUSIVE interview with "Albert the Astronomer."

DARLENE *(right behind* COLLEEN*):* Yeah, right. An EXCLUSIVE interview with "Albert the Astronomer."

ALBERT: Correctomundo, ladies. Well, actually that's not one hundred percent accurate. It won't be an EXCLUSIVE interview.

COLLEEN: See? What did I tell you, Darlene?

(COLLEEN *and* DARLENE *laugh.)*

ALBERT: There will be correspondents from other networks there as well. *(Now in shock,* COLLEEN *and* DARLENE *stop laughing and go back to their "away place.")* NBC, ABC, CNN, PBS, CBN, and—oh, I can NEVER remember the call letters of that one in Nashville.

STEVE: TNN?

ALBERT: Yes, I think that's the one.

BUBBA: TNN? TNN?!

NANCY: Why would a country music station be doing a story on the comet?

ALBERT: I asked myself the same question. But after giving it considerable thought, I realized that many country music lyrics deal with disaster and superstition.

BETSY *(joins the group, speaking dreamily):* And romance.

ALBERT: Yes, romance. I think that goes without saying.

STEVE: So what's that got to do with the comet?

ALBERT: Since the first sightings, we earthlings have always been awed by the brilliance and seemingly erratic movement of the comet. The common observer is often gripped by fear or even terror upon sighting a comet. In fact, a comet was thought to be an omen or warning of certain events, usually disasters, such as wars or famines or deaths of kings.

BETSY: And didn't the Greeks believe that comets had mystical powers of love too?

ALBERT: While it's true that the word "comet" originates from the Greek term for "hairy star," I do not recollect any data concerning the comet possessing powers of love. However, it's entirely possible. The ancient Greeks were known to be superstitious. Especially in the area of romance.

GLORIA *(joins the group):* "Hairy star." NOW I get it! "HAIRY star"—THAT'S why you're supposed to put a lock of HAIR under your pillow.

(BETSY *motions* GLORIA *to keep quiet.*)

NANCY: Why would you put a lock of your hair under your pillow?

GLORIA: No, silly. Not a lock of your own hair. You're supposed to get a lock of hair from someone you love. Betsy says if you put it under your pillow the night of a comet, then that person will fall in love with you!

BETSY: Gloria! Don't you need to go home and practice for the talent show?

GLORIA: No.

BETSY: Well, don't you need to try on your costume to see if it still fits?

GLORIA: No.

BETSY: Are you sure? You've lost weight since last year's show.

GLORIA *(flattered):* Really? Do you really think so?

BETSY: Yeah. Your mom might need to take it in a few inches.

GLORIA *(feels hips):* Wow. Maybe you're right. I guess all those hula lessons are finally starting to pay off. I'd better call Mom and tell her to pick me up. *(She moves to phone.)*

NANCY *(to* BETSY*):* A lock of hair under a pillow?

BETSY *(nervously laughs):* Oh, you know Gloria. She tends to exaggerate sometimes. So, Albert! Tell us about the interviews with the media!

ALBERT: Quite routine, actually.

BUBBA: Albert, tell me you're not joking. TNN?!

ALBERT: You got it, Kemosabe. And I managed to put in a good word for you.

BUBBA: Whoa. You mean you talked to TNN about ME?

ALBERT: Exactamundo. I told them about the comet song you wrote.

BUBBA: And?

ALBERT: And how you're going to sing it at the talent show tonight with your country western band.

BUBBA: And?

ALBERT: And they said they'd meet me there tonight.

BUBBA: Really? TNN is going to hear me sing tonight?

ALBERT: That's a big ten-four, little buddy.

BUBBA: I can't believe it. This is the big break I've been waiting for. TNN wants to hear ME sing!

ALBERT: Well, actually, they didn't say they want to hear you sing. Not in so many words.

STEVE: I thought you said they're coming to the talent show.

ALBERT: This is correct. But what I neglected to mention is that my hay fever acted up during our interview, so I suggested that we finish the interview at the school gym tonight.

BUBBA: Albert, you don't have hay fever.

ALBERT: You know that, and I know that, but THEY don't know that. I had to think up some ruse to get them to hear your band tonight. Listen to this—*(He fakes a sneeze.)* I'm considering a second career as an actor.

BUBBA: Thanks, buddy.

ALBERT: Ah, don't mention it. What are friends for?

STEVE: Reality check, Bubba. How're you gonna get off work early? Luigi's never gonna let you go when he's got this many customers.

BUBBA: I'm way ahead of you. Sarah Littleton gave me the flu.

BUFFY: She did? You know she had such a high fever that her skin got all blotchy. She couldn't even cover it up with makeup.

BUBBA: No, she didn't give me the flu. That's just what I'm gonna tell Uncle Gino.

STEVE: You're gonna lie to Gino?

BUBBA: It's not really a lie. I went out with Sarah last Saturday night. Maybe she gave me the flu and I just don't have any symptoms yet.

STEVE *(walks backward, away from BUBBA)*: I just don't want to be around when Gino and Luigi find out the truth.

BUBBA: Hey! They're not gonna know 'cause nobody's gonna tell 'em, right?

GINO *(enters from kitchen, mopping brow with napkin)*: Whew! Finally. The lasagna. It's ready.

JERRY *(eager and hungry):* Lasagna?

GINO *(puts arm around* JERRY*):* Ey—Jerry. I'm about to make you an offer you cannot refuse. How would you like some free lasagna?

JERRY: What's the catch?

GINO: You serve my customers their lasagna, and then I serve you your lasagna. Deal?

JERRY: Deal.

GINO: That goes for all the rest of you kids. Hurry—my customers are waiting!

BUBBA: Uncle Gino?

GINO: What is it, Bubba?

BUBBA: Uh—I don't feel so hot.

GINO: Later, Bubba, later. I got hungry customers waiting. *(He ushers everyone into kitchen.* BETSY *is at the end of the pack.)* Faster. Mach schnell!

NANCY: Mach schnell?

GINO: So I watch *Hogan's Heroes* reruns, all right?

GLORIA *(looks out window):* There's my mom! Hey, Betsy! I'll see you at the talent show! Good luck getting Bubba's hair! *(She exits.)*

GINO *(to* BETSY*):* Bubba's hair?

BETSY *(nervously laughs):* It's a long story, Gino, and you have hungry customers, remember?

*(*GINO *and* BETSY *follow everyone into kitchen.)*

(The actors serve the customers lasagna between **Scene 3** *and* **Scene 4**.*)*

Scene 4
"But My Stomach Doesn't Speak Italian"

(JERRY *and* BUFFY *are seated at their table.* NANCY, MARIA, *and* ALBERT *are next to the table, talking.* COLLEEN, DARLENE, *and* BUBBA *are talking at one end of the room.* LUIGI, BETSY, JONATHAN, RUSTY, *and* DAVE *are in the kitchen.* GLORIA *is outside.* GINO *is refilling a customer's glass.*)

JERRY: Yo, Luigi!

LUIGI *(enters from kitchen):* EY!

JERRY: Where's the lasagna Gino promised me?

LUIGI: Whatza matter for you, eh? *(He exits to kitchen.)*

GINO: A thousand apologies, my friend. I had no idea there would be so many customers! Luigi must've run out.

NANCY: I've never seen this many people in town. Not even for the Fourth of July parade.

ALBERT: You're absolutely right, Nancy. I estimate that our town's population has increased by approximately 143 percent, not including the television crews.

NANCY: Wow. All because of a comet.

JERRY: Yeah, well, my stomach doesn't care about a comet. It wants lasagna!

GINO: Jerry, my friend. We have a little saying in Italy for when things don't go so good: "Che sara, sara."

JERRY: My stomach doesn't understand Italian.

GINO: Come on, Jerry. With as much meatballs and pizza and pasta and spumoni that your stomach has seen—I bet it could speak better Italian than my own mother. But I tell you what I'm gonna do for you. You and Buffy will be my special guests next Friday night, table for two, candlelight dinner. I'll even arrange for my cousin, Carmine, to serenade you with his accordion.

BUFFY: That sounds great! Doesn't that sound great, Jerry? What time?

ALBERT *(looks at watch)*: The time is 2:54 A.M.

NANCY: Two fifty-four A.M.?! You have REALLY flipped, Albert!

ALBERT *(pushing buttons on watch)*: Of course, that's the time in Hong Kong. Did I fail to mention that? I can also supply you with the time and temperature of our present location.

BUFFY: No. I know what time it is here. I was asking Gino what time we're supposed to come next Friday night.

BETSY *(joins the group)*: What's going on next Friday night?

BUFFY: Gino invited us for a candlelight dinner. With an accordion player serenading us.

BETSY: How romantic.

COLLEEN *(strolling past BETSY to other side of room)*: ACCORDION player? How gauche. Does he bring his little monkey too?

DARLENE *(right behind COLLEEN)*: Yeah, how gauche. Does he bring his little monkey too?

GINO: For your information, my cousin, Carmine, studied accordion with the great Domenic Pizarro. And when Carmine plays "The Flight of the Bumblebee," ah—you must have your fire extinguisher ready to put out the smoke.

BUFFY: That sounds great! Doesn't that sound great, Jerry? So what time should we get here?

JONATHAN *(joins the group)*: What time are we supposed to be here for what?

NANCY: Gino's having a candlelight dinner next Friday night.

JONATHAN *(puts arm around GINO)*: Hey—my man, Gino. You really know how to do this appreciation thing up right. You know . . . *(he strolls as he philosophizes)* expressing gratitude doesn't come easy for a lot of people. Maybe they see it as a sign of weakness. Unfortunately, our society is impressed with the guy at the top of the ladder—we don't care how he got there. And we tend to look down on the nice guy, down there on rung number two. But he's the one boosting everyone up to the third rung. *(He turns, dramatically, and points.)* That should tell us something about the human condition.

GINO: But—

GLORIA *(enters from outside):* Hey, Betsy! You were wrong about my costume for the talent show. It fits just fine. It's a good thing too. I don't think you can take in the seams on a grass skirt. As a matter of fact, I don't think there ARE any seams in a grass skirt. It's just basically *(pauses and thinks)* grass. Oh well. Did you get a lock of Bubba's hair yet?

BETSY: GLORIA! You're interrupting. It's not polite to interrupt, you know. *(To* BUFFY*)* Go ahead, Buffy.

BUFFY: Go ahead with what?

BETSY: You were asking Gino what time to come for the candlelight dinner next Friday night.

GLORIA: Really? A candlelight dinner? Is everybody invited? Can I come too, Gino?

GINO: Why not. I tell you what—you kids come next Friday after the game and Luigi and I will prepare a feast. *(Pause)* But—uh—let's don't tell Luigi about it just yet. We still have to take care of all these customers. Deal?

EVERYONE: Deal!

GLORIA: Just think, Betsy. If you can get Bubba's hair under your pillow tonight, then I bet you two little lovebirds will be sitting at a table for two next Friday night!

BETSY: GLORIA!

COLLEEN *(crosses in front of* BETSY *and walks back to* BUBBA*):* Really, Betsy. WhatEVER gave you the idea that YOU are Bubba's type?

DARLENE *(follows* COLLEEN*):* Yeah, Betsy. WhatEVER gave you the idea that YOU are Bubba's type?

BETSY: Thanks, Gloria. Now everybody knows.

ALBERT: Correction, Betsy. Everyone ALREADY knew, long ago. In fact, we've all known about your obsession with Bubba for eleven months now.

JONATHAN: Yeah, don't feel bad, Betsy. You're not the only one.

MARIA: You mean you have a crush on Bubba too?

JONATHAN: No, I mean that Betsy's not the only man-chaser. Women have been chasing men since the beginning of time. Cleopatra chased Anthony, Potiphar's wife chased Joseph, Lucy chased Ricky, Roxie chased Larry [substitute names of a favorite couple in your church, or JONATHAN's real parents].

NANCY *(interrupts):* Who's Roxie? [or substitute name]

JONATHAN: ~~My mom.~~ The Pastor's wife. As I was saying . . . *(he strolls as he philosophizes)* the male and female of our species have been playing mind games for so long, they've forgotten how to enjoy an open, honest relationship. We're a generation that's been brought up on soap operas. So it shouldn't surprise us that one out of every three marriages in America ends in divorce. *(He turns, dramatically, and points.)* That should tell us something about the human condition.

BETSY: It's OK, Jonathan. I've just about given up anyway. Bubba and I will never be anything more than just friends. Colleen and Darlene are right. I am definitely NOT Bubba's type.

GINO: Please forgive me for butting in like this, Betsy, but I think you stare too much at the flowers.

BETSY: What?

GINO: It's just a little something my mama used to say to me over and over again. She'd say, "Gino *(picks up a plastic flower from a vase on a table, admiring it),* you think if you stare at one flower long enough—you can make it bloom? (He slaps the flower with the palm of his hand.) Whatza matter for you, ey? (He yells at flower.)* With all this time you waste staring at one flower, you could be planting 20 more! It's not your job to make the flower bloom . . . *(he looks heavenward)* that's the work of our God in heaven. Your job, my little Gino, is to tend to ALL of God's creation, and to give HIM thanks for the flowers that DO bloom!

BETSY: I get it. Like, "there's other fish in the sea." So, I should be chasing—I mean "pursuing"—other guys besides just Bubba. Kinda like diversifying my investments.

MARIA: Uncle Gino?

GINO: Yes, what is it, Maria?

MARIA: That's a plastic flower.

GINO: I know this, Maria.

MARIA: Plastic flowers don't bloom.

GINO: MARIA! *(He throws her a kiss with both hands.)* You have said it perfectly! Man cannot make as beautiful a flower as God. Betsy—do not spend your time trying to make a flower on your own. *(He returns flower to vase.)* Spend time with the Master Gardener—the Creator—and tend to the garden HE gives you.

JONATHAN: So, you're saying that human relationships are like flowers. *(He thinks about it.)* You know, our society has carried the do-it-yourself philosophy to the extreme. We've even tried creating LOVE on our own. *(He picks up artificial flower and contemplates it.)* There's nothing special about a man-made flower. But natural, God-made flowers take time to cultivate. And they smell out of this world. *(He thinks about it.)* Flowers. *(He thinks about it.)* I like it.

GINO: Thank you, Jonathan.

BETSY: Oh, now I get it.

JONATHAN: There's just one thing, though. A real flower eventually dies. But plastic flowers don't even decompose—they last forever.

GINO: Jonathan . . . *(he takes flower from JONATHAN and places it back in vase)* my friend, my fellow philosopher. *(He puts arm around JONATHAN and walks him to Mama's picture.)* You remind me of something else my mama used to say to me: *(Turns to him and yells)* "Whatza matter for you, eh? You THINK too much!"

BUBBA *(approaches* GINO*)*: Uncle Gino—

GINO: Yes, Bubba.

BUBBA: I don't feel so good. Maybe I should clock out early.

RUSTY *(enters from kitchen):* Hey, Albert!

ALBERT: Present and accounted for.

RUSTY: We saw you on TV! Just now in the kitchen! You were doing a commercial!

COLLEEN: Albert doing a commercial. *(She laughs.)* What were you advertising, Albert—pocket protectors for your pens?

DARLENE: Yeah, what were you advertising, Albert—pocket protectors for your pens?

RUSTY: No, he wasn't selling anything. It's a commercial for the news. Albert's going to be on channel 7 news!

BUBBA *(puts arm around* ALBERT*)*: Congratulations, Albert! Yo, Uncle Gino—*(He starts to leave with* ALBERT*.)* I'm going to take Albert home so we can catch him on the news. I'll be back later.

RUSTY: Luigi's got a TV in the kitchen.

GINO: That's right, Bubba. You stay here.

BUBBA *(turns back):* Thanks a lot, Rusty.

RUSTY: Sure thing, Bubba. I thought I'd save you the trip. *(He returns to kitchen, tripping over beverage table on his way.)*

BUBBA: Speaking of trips.

GINO: Albert! This is exciting news! You didn't tell me you were a celebrity!

JONATHAN: Andy Warhol said that the day will come when everyone will be famous for 15 seconds

BUFFY *(jumps up and paces nervously):* Oh, Jerry! What if TONIGHT'S going to be MY 15 seconds of fame? What if the TV cameras focus on the top of the human pyramid for 15 seconds? Oh, Jerry—I am soooo nervous.

JERRY: Don't worry. You'll do great, Babe.

BUFFY: But, Jerry! What if I fall off before my 15 seconds of fame are up? What am I going to do?

JERRY *(gets up and ushers* BUFFY *back to her seat)*: Don't worry. You'll do great, Babe.

ALBERT: As I recollect, Andy Warhol said everyone will be famous for 15 MINUTES, not 15 SECONDS.

JONATHAN *(shrugs shoulders)*: All time is relative.

GINO: So, Albert. Tell me about the television news.

ALBERT: There's really not that much to tell. Various television reporters interviewed me concerning my blue ribbon science project on the origin, evolution, and configuration of the comet.

HI MADELINE

GLORIA: My mother says that a comet means the end of the world is near.

NANCY: Really? You mean the world could end tonight?

ALBERT: Highly improbable. Scientists have been spotting comets for centuries, and the earth is still standing. Well, actually, the earth does not "stand," it rotates on its axis.

NANCY: But what if THIS comet is "THE" comet?

STEVE: Yeah. What if the world DOES end tonight?

BUFFY: I can't believe it. *(She gets up and paces nervously.)* I'll have my 15 seconds of fame on top of the human pyramid, and then—POOF! I'll be gone. That just doesn't seem fair.

JERRY: Don't worry. You'll do great, Babe.

ALBERT: And remember, Buffy—it's 15 MINUTES, not seconds.

BUFFY: WhatEVER!

JERRY *(gets up and tries to usher* BUFFY *back to table)*: Don't worry. You'll do great, Babe.

BUFFY *(resisting)*: But what difference is it going to make if I POOF?

GINO: Buffy—don't you realize that you or I or any of us could POOF at any moment, with or without a comet?

BUFFY: No. (JERRY *ushers* BUFFY *back to her seat.*)

JONATHAN *(strolling as he philosophizes)*: Today's society is into heavy denial about our own mortality. We use wrinkle-free cream to mask our aging skin. We use dyes to color our gray hair. We have a hard time accepting the fact that none of us will live forever. *(He turns, dramatically, and points.)* That should tell us something about the human condition.

GINO: Ah, my friend, but that's where you are wrong. We CAN live forever.

NANCY: I thought you said that we're going to POOF at any moment.

GINO: Yes, indeed. But the Holy Scriptures say Jesus Christ died for us so that we may LIVE together with Him.

DAVE *(enters from kitchen)*: Yo, Gino! Dessert's ready!

GINO: Mama mia! I almost forgot! The customers! We need to serve the desserts!

DAVE: I'll bring the desserts out for you. *(He turns and trips on his way to kitchen.)*

GINO: Quick! All you kids get the desserts before Dave does!

(Everyone exits to kitchen, with BETSY, GLORIA, *and* GINO *at the end of the pack.* MARIA *stays put.)*

GINO: Hey, Betsy. You think about what we talked about, eh?

BETSY: I already thought about it. You're right, Gino. I need to spend more time thinking about God, and less time thinking about boys.

GINO: That's my girl.

MARIA: Hey Betsy.

BETSY *(to* MARIA*)*: Yeah?

(BETSY *and* GLORIA *turn back as* GINO *follows others to kitchen.*)

MARIA: How come you want some of Bubba's hair?

BETSY: Oh, it was just a silly superstition that the comet had special powers of love, that's all.

MARIA: So did you get any?

BETSY: Any what?

MARIA: Hair. Bubba's hair.

BETSY: No. I'm not going to TRY to get anyone to fall in love with me anymore. I'm just going to be myself from now on.

MARIA: Oh. So you don't want it?

BETSY: Want what?

MARIA: Hair. Bubba's hair! And people think I'M a space cadet. I'm asking you if you want to borrow a lock of Bubba's hair.

BETSY: Borrow?

MARIA: Yeah. You can't keep it. It's in our family scrapbook. It's from his first haircut.

BETSY: Wow! And you mean I could borrow it tonight, and put it under my pillow during the comet?!

MARIA: Isn't that what I've been saying?

BETSY: C'mon, let's go get it now!

GLORIA: But, Betsy—I thought you said it was a silly superstition.

BETSY: I don't care. I'll try ANYTHING to get Bubba to fall in love with me!

GLORIA: But, Betsy—you said you're not going to try to get anyone to fall in love with you anymore.

BETSY: GLORIA! Here's the deal—keep your mouth shut and you can come, OK?

GLORIA *(says "OK" with lips shut):* Mmph-mmph.

[handwritten: ABUSE ME MADELINE!]

BETSY *(to* MARIA *as the three girls exit to outside):* So you REALLY have a lock of Bubba's hair? REALLY?!

MARIA: Isn't that what I've been saying?

(The rest of the cast serves the desserts between **Scene 4** *and* **Scene 5**.*)*

Scene 5
"Apocalypse, Now?!"

(RUSTY *and* LUIGI *are in the kitchen.* MARIA, GLORIA, *and* BETSY *are outside.* DAVE *is talking to* MARYANNE. *The rest of the cast are in the room.)*

RUSTY *(enters from kitchen):* Yo, Albert! Hurry! *(He trips.)* They just said you're on after the next commercial break!

BUBBA *(puts arm around* ALBERT *as they go to kitchen):* Way to go, Albert!

(Everyone exits to kitchen. GINO *is at the end of the crowd.)*

*(*MARIA *and* GLORIA *enter from outside.)*

GINO *(turns):* Maria! Where have you been?

MARIA: Uhmm. When?

GINO: Just now when we were serving the desserts!

MARIA: Uhmm. Desserts?

GINO: Maria. Do I give you a paycheck for working here as a waitress?

MARIA: Uhmm. Is this a trick question?

STEVE *(enters from kitchen):* Yo, Gino! You're gonna miss Albert!

GINO *(to* MARIA*)*: Never mind. We talk later. Come! Our little Albert is about to become a Hollywood television star!

(MARIA, GLORIA, STEVE *and* GINO *exit to kitchen.)*

BETSY *(enters from outside):* Thanks, Maria. It's all set. *(She looks around.)* Maria? Gloria? I must have beat them back. *(Beat)* But we all left Maria's house at the same time, and it must've taken me at least five, maybe seven minutes to get to my house and put Bubba's hair under my pillow. They definitely should have gotten back first. *(Beat. Reassures herself.)* I bet they stopped at Gloria's house to look at her grass skirt. She's so proud of that thing. *(Beat. Apprehensive.)* No, Gloria lives on the other end of town. *(Beat. Looks around.)* And where's everybody else? *(She yells.)* Yo, Luigi! *(She waits for answer, then panics.)* Oh no! *(Beat. She tries to calm herself.)* No, this is really crazy. *(Beat)* This can NOT be the end of the world. I mean, I wouldn't still be here if it were the end of the world, right? *(Beat. Reassures herself.)* Right. *(Beat. She starts to panic.)* But what if they all POOFED and I didn't? What if God only POOFS people that believe in Him, and He leaves the rest of us down here to suffer? *(Beat. Justifies herself.)* But I believe in God! *(Beat. Reassures herself.)* Yeah, I believe in God. *(Beat. She starts to panic.)* So then what if God only POOFS people that read the Bible? *(Beat. Justifies herself.)* But I read the Bible! In fact, I have some of it memorized. Well, maybe two verses. But that's a start! I know John 3:16. "For God so loved the world, that he gave his only begotten Son, that whosoever believeth in him should not perish, but have everlasting life." And I know 1 Thessalonians 5:26. That's my favorite. "Greet the BRETHREN with a holy kiss." *(Beat. She realizes her falling short.)* But that's all I know. *(Beat. Angry at self.)* Oh man, I have REALLY blown it. I can tell you Bubba's class schedule for the last three years. You pick any day this month, and I can tell you what shirt and pants and shoes he wore that day. *(Beat. Panics.)* But what good's that gonna do me when it's time to be POOFED? I know TWO lousy Bible verses. *(Beat. She picks flowers out of vase.)* Gino was right. I've been spending all my time trying to make my own, artificial flowers . . . *(she throws them down, disgusted)* and they're no good. *(Beat. She stares at flowers.)* Figures. I never HAVE been good at arts and crafts. *(Beat. A spark of hope.)* Wait a minute! There couldn't have been a POOF! *(She gestures to audience.)* YOU'RE all still here! *(Beat. Her smile turns to a frown as she assesses the audience.)* No. You don't look like the "holy" type. You've probably been left here to suffer just like me. *(Beat)* I can't believe I wasted my whole life. And that's it. No second chances. Once you miss the POOF, it's too late.

COLLEEN *(enters from kitchen and walks to her table):* Big hairy deal. So Albert gets to be on TV for some geeky science project. Like I care.

DARLENE *(right behind* COLLEEN*)*: Yeah, so Albert gets to be on TV for some geeky science project. Like I care. (COLLEEN *and* DARLENE *sit.)*

(The rest of the kids enter from kitchen. JERRY *and* BUFFY *sit at their table.* DAVE *follows close behind* MARYANNE. BETSY *greets all of them with enthusiastic hugs, even* COLLEEN *and* DARLENE, *as* BUBBA *speaks.)*

BUBBA: Good job, Albert. You had poise.

STEVE: Weren't you nervous?

ALBERT: Actually, I was so absorbed in the facts of the comet that I forgot about my own insecurities.

STEVE: So weren't you nervous?

BUBBA: He said no.

STEVE: Oh. *(He walks to an "away place.")*

BETSY: You guys! You're all here!

MARIA: Yeah? Where are we supposed to be?

BETSY: But where were you? I yelled for Luigi.

NANCY: We heard you. But Albert was on TV.

BETSY: So you didn't get POOFED!

MARIA: Uhmm. *(She looks around.)* No, I don't think so.

BETSY: Yo, Luigi!

LUIGI *(enters from kitchen):* EY!

BETSY: Nothing. Just testing. Thanks!

LUIGI: Whatza matter for you, eh? *(He exits to kitchen.)*

BETSY: This is great! It's like—like getting a second chance after all!

BUBBA: Betsy, are you all right? You've been acting crazy all day. First the deal with the scissors, and now you're not making any sense at all.

BETSY: No, now I AM making sense. Finally.

BUBBA: See what I mean?

BUFFY *(approaches* BUBBA): Bubba, are you going to leave soon? I really need the extra practice.

BUBBA: Yeah. Give me five minutes. I just need to tell Gino.

BUFFY: You're going to tell Gino about the talent show?

BUBBA: Are you crazy?! I'm gonna tell him I'm sick.

BUFFY: I'm sorry. I hope you feel better in time to sing with your band.

BUBBA: JER-RY!

JERRY *(approaches* BUBBA): Gotcha. *(He puts arm around* BUFFY *and leads her back to their table.)* Don't worry. You'll do great, Babe.

GLORIA: Hey, Betsy—you missed watching Albert on TV. He was FASCINATING!

ALBERT: Why, thank you, Gloria.

GLORIA: Except I don't know WHY you had to say that part about a comet having GAS. I mean, a lot of people eat dinner while they're watching the news, and I don't think they want to hear about GAS.

52

ALBERT: But gas is one of the basic components of a comet, Gloria. The nucleus releases both dust and gas through the action of solar radiation.

GLORIA: There you go again. NOW you're talking about GAS in a restaurant!

ALBERT: But, Gloria—

BUBBA: Give it up, Albert.

ALBERT: Right.

NANCY: Albert—do you really think we'll be able to see the comet without telescopes?

ALBERT: We have records of comet sightings by Aristotle in the fourth century B.C., and even before that in the Chinese annals. They go back more than 3,000 years. I doubt if these astronomical spotters had access to the modern technology that we use today.

NANCY: So we could just go outside and look up at the sky and see it?

ALBERT: If the conditions are right.

MARYANNE: I wouldn't know WHAT to look for. I don't even know where the North Star is.

DAVE: Maryanne . . . *(he tries to look cool by placing his hand on the table* [or wall] *behind* MARYANNE *and leaning toward her)* I can show you a whole new world. *(He uses grand gestures with his free hand.)* Shimmering, shiny, and splendid. But . . . *(he touches her face and leans closer)* don't you dare close your eyes. *(His hand slips off the table* [or wall] *and he falls on the floor.)*

ALBERT *(to* MARYANNE *as he steps over* DAVE*)*: If you'd like, I could go out with you and point it out.

MARYANNE: Yeah, that'd be great. Let me go ask Gino if I can take a break. *(She exits to kitchen.)*

STEVE *(helps* DAVE *up)*: Here, let me give you a hand.

DAVE: I don't get it. I've tried EVERYTHING I know. I used ALL the right lines. Just like in the movies.

STEVE: Dave—you got that line from a Disney movie.

DAVE: Aladdin ended up marrying Princess Jasmine, am I right?

STEVE: This is worse than I thought. C'mon. Let's get you some fresh air.

(STEVE *and* DAVE *start to go outside. The other kids follow.*)

GINO *(enters from kitchen):* Ey! Where do you think you're going?

NANCY *(turning back):* We're going to look at the comet.

GINO: I know this. What I DON'T know is why you would desert your good friend, Gino, when he needs to refill all these customers' drinks!

(Everyone turns and walks back to kitchen. BUBBA *approaches* GINO.*)*

BUBBA: Uncle Gino?

GINO: What is it, Bubba?

BUBBA: I don't feel so good.

GINO: You don't feel so good. Of COURSE you don't feel so good. Sarah Littleton gave you the flu.

BUBBA *(surprised):* Yeah. That's right.

GINO: So maybe you should go home and get some sleep.

BUBBA: Yeah. OK. Thanks. *(He starts to leave.)*

GINO: You want that I should call the boys in your country western band and tell them the bad news for you?

BUBBA *(stops dead in his tracks):* Huh?

GINO: The terrible news that their lead singer is too sick to sing in the talent show tonight.

BUBBA: Uh—look, Uncle Gino—uh—I was just—uh—well, I needed to—uh—

GINO: Say no more, Bubba. You've said plenty already. First we fill the customers' drinks, then we talk—you and me and Luigi.

BUBBA: POP? Why do we have to bring Pop into this?

GINO: Later, Bubba. I have customers. (GINO *and* BUBBA *exit to kitchen.*)

(The cast refills the customers' drinks between **Scene 5** *and* **Scene 6**.*)*

Scene 6
"Whatza Matter for You, Eh?"

(Before the scene starts, BETSY *should already be outside.* LUIGI *and* GINO *are in the kitchen. The scene starts with the teens exiting to the outside as a group to see the comet.* BUBBA *and* STEVE *are at the end of the group.)*

GINO *(enters from kitchen)*: Bubba! Where do you think you're going?

BUBBA: Out to see the comet. *(He continues to exit.)*

GINO *(screams)*: Luciano Vincent Anthony DiDonato!

(Everyone freezes.)

NANCY *(warily)*: What's the English translation for what he just said?

ALBERT: There is no translation. That was Bubba's full name.

NANCY *(relieved)*: Good. Then WE'RE not in trouble.

(Everyone except STEVE, BUBBA *and* GINO *exits.)*

STEVE *(to* BUBBA*)*: Luciano?

BUBBA: Yeah. That's what my mom named me. She wanted me to be a great opera singer. You know, like Pavarotti.

GINO *(pulls out chair, turning it sideways)*: We talk. NOW!

STEVE: See ya. *(He exits.)*

BUBBA *(to* STEVE*)*: Traitor. *(He sits in chair.)*

GINO: Yo, Luigi!

LUIGI *(enters from kitchen):* EY!

GINO *(pulls out other chair, turning it sideways, facing* BUBBA*'s chair):* We talk.

LUIGI: Whatza matter for you, eh?

GINO *(points to chair):* We talk. NOW!

(LUIGI *reluctantly sits in chair.* BUBBA *and* LUIGI *appear uncomfortable during some moments of awkward silence.)*

GINO *(finally breaks the silence)*: I said, we talk.

BUBBA: Yeah?

GINO: So talk!

BUBBA: Talk about what?

GINO: Talk about why you don't talk.

BUBBA: There's nothing to talk about.

GINO: A boy needs to talk to his father.

BUBBA: And what if the boy's father doesn't talk to him? Then what, Uncle Gino? What if the boy has never heard his father say, "I love you, Son," or "I'm proud of you, Son."

LUIGI *(lovingly to* BUBBA*)*: Whatza matter for you, eh?

GINO: Did you hear that?

BUBBA: Yeah.

GINO: You don't call that love?

BUBBA: Do YOU?

GINO: You know whatza matter for you, Bubba? You know why you don't HEAR? Because you don't LISTEN, that's why! Luigi's worked hard to be a father AND a mother to you and Maria ever since your mama passed away. You think it was easy for him when you kids would have nightmares and call out for your mama in the middle of the night? You think he didn't want to call out for her too? And then he cooks and cleans and helps you with your homework and takes you to the doctor and THEN—he starts a catering business on the side so he can pay for the voice lessons your mama wanted you to have. And do you THANK Luigi for all these things? Do you say, "Thank you, Papa, for the roof over my head and the food on my table"? Do you say, "Thank you, Papa, for my voice lessons"? NO! You know what you do? You send your friend, Albert, in your place to your voice lessons while you practice with your country western band. Do you think that we are THAT stupid?

BUBBA: How did you know?

GINO: I KNOW these things. But what I DON'T know is why you lie to your papa and to your Uncle Gino.

BUBBA: I didn't really lie.

GINO: Luciano!

BUBBA: OK, so I stretched the truth a little. I knew Pop would never let me sing in a country western band.

GINO: And HOW do you know this?

BUBBA: They named me Luciano. Does that give you any clue?

GINO: Your mama named you Luciano because she knew you would be a great singer.

BUBBA: So why did Pop sign me up for opera lessons?

GINO: Maybe because that's all Luigi knows. Maybe he doesn't know about any other voice lessons because maybe YOU don't tell him.

LUIGI *(lovingly to* BUBBA*)*: Whatza matter for you, eh?

GINO: See?

BUBBA: So now what?

GINO: Now we look at the comet.

LUIGI *(aggravated at* GINO*)*: Whatza matter for you, eh?

GINO: Luigi, for once you're gonna do what your little brother Gino says. Come. We look at the comet.

BUBBA: Then what?

GINO *(philosophically):* Then—we will consider the heavens, the work of God's own fingers. We will gaze upon the moon and the stars which He has set in place. We will wonder at the comet as it writes the signature of God in the sky. And we will realize that we are so tiny—so very, very small.

BUBBA: And?

GINO *(back on earth):* And that we could POOF at any moment. Better that a father and his son should POOF with love and trust in their hearts, capisce?

BUBBA *(resigned):* Capisce.

(The teens enter from the outside.)

GLORIA: Wow. That was incredible. Do you think it's a sign?

BETSY: More like an exclamation point.

ALBERT: I think you mean the coma, Betsy. There are three basic components of a comet—the nucleus, the tail, and the COMA. No exclamation point, I'm afraid.

BETSY: For me it was an exclamation point.

JONATHAN: That's interesting. I used to think of the heavens as a question mark. But now I see what Betsy's talking about. It's definitely an exclamation point. Like Michelangelo's painting of God's hand reaching down and touching the fingers of humanity. *(He pauses and thinks.)* Like . . . *(he turns dramatically and points)* maybe there IS hope for the human condition, after all.

GINO: Come—Bubba, Luigi. We shall see it for ourselves.

(BUBBA *and* GINO *start to exit to outside.* LUIGI *stays in chair.*)

GINO *(stops and turns):* Yo, Luigi!

LUIGI: EY!

GINO: You'll come?

LUIGI: Whatza matter for you, eh? *(He gets up and walks toward kitchen door.)*

GINO: For me and for Bubba.

(LUIGI *keeps walking to kitchen.*)

GINO: For ROSA!

(LUIGI *stops.*)

GINO: Come, my brother. We do it for Rosa—eh?

(LUIGI *turns and walks to* GINO, *who puts his arms around* LUIGI *and* BUBBA *as they exit to outside.*)

BUFFY: Jerry, how long do you think Bubba's going to take? I REALLY need to get to the gym and practice.

JERRY: C'mon. I'll drop you off.

BUFFY: But the gym's on the other end of town. Don't you have to go home and get changed?

JERRY: Yeah, but I gotta eat something too. Bulky Burgers is down the street from the gym. I'll get the El Grande to go.

BUFFY: Just make sure you don't get the spicy fries. Remember how your ears turned red the last time?

JERRY: Yeah, yeah. C'mon—let's go, Babe.

(JERRY *and* BUFFY *exit to outside.*)

BETSY *(hands* MARIA *a plastic bag with hair in it):* Here, Maria. Thanks.

MARIA *(takes bag):* You're welcome. *(Looks at bag and drops it)* Gross, Betsy! What IS this?

BETSY *(picks up bag and hands it to* MARIA*)*: It's Bubba's hair. You gave it to me, remember?

MARIA: Uhmm—I do?

GLORIA: Maria! We went to your house and got it out of your family scrapbook!

MARIA: Oh, yeah. So?

BETSY: So, I'm returning it.

MARIA: Why?

BETSY: Because I don't need it anymore.

GLORIA: Did it work already?

BETSY: No. Something ELSE worked already. *(Confidently)* I decided to get out of the flower-making business.

GLORIA: I'm confused.

MARIA: Boy, am I glad to hear somebody ELSE say that.

GINO *(enters from outside):* Hey, everybody! Who's gonna go to the talent show?

(Everyone is silent.)

GINO: It's OK. I know about the talent show.

(Everyone remains silent.)

GINO: So let me put it this way—I am gonna hear Bubba sing. And I am gonna take the catering van. So who wants a ride to the gym?

(JONATHAN, BETSY, GLORIA, NANCY, STEVE, MARIA, ALBERT, MARYANNE, DAVE, *and* RUSTY *accept the offer.)*

COLLEEN *(sashays to other side of room):* Me? Ride in a catering van? No way!

DARLENE *(right behind* COLLEEN*)*: Yeah, a catering van? No way!

GINO: Colleen. I would consider it an honor and a privilege for someone of your impeccable taste to accompany me to the school gym in my van.

COLLEEN *(stops and turns toward* GINO*)*: Really?

DARLENE *(same as* COLLEEN*)*: Yeah, really?

GINO: On one condition. You all must think of something nice to say about each passenger.

COLLEEN: You have GOT to be kidding.

DARLENE: Yeah, you have GOT to be kidding.

GINO: I will start. Colleen—you have the makings of a leader. Use this gift for good, and you will lead many people to the truth.

(COLLEEN *stares at* GINO, *dumbfounded.*)

GINO: And, Darlene—you have the gift of support. Use this power for good, and you will strengthen many.

(DARLENE *stares at* GINO, *dumbfounded.*)

GINO: See how much fun this is? *(He ushers everyone outside, including* COLLEEN *and* DARLENE. BETSY *is at the end of the group.)* Who's gonna go next?

(BUBBA *and* LUIGI *enter as everyone starts to exit.* LUIGI *goes to kitchen.)*

GINO: Bubba! Luigi! Come—we take the van to the gym.

BUBBA: You go on, Uncle Gino. We'll take my car.

GINO: Bueno. *(He exits, yelling to the teens who are already outside.)* So whose turn is it to say something nice, eh?

BUBBA: Yo, Betsy.

BETSY *(turns before she exits):* Yeah?

BUBBA: You need a ride to the gym?

BETSY: No thanks. I told Gino I'd go in the van.

BUBBA: But you could go with me in my car.

BETSY: I know. Thanks anyway.

BUBBA *(can't believe she turned him down):* Are you feeling OK?

BETSY: Yeah. I feel great.

BUBBA: Well, maybe we can get together sometime. Maybe tomorrow?

BETSY: Tomorrow? Uh—I kinda have plans tomorrow.

BUBBA: What're you doing?

BETSY: There's a meeting at church. I was kinda thinking about going.

BUBBA: Oh. So maybe I could take you and—we could go out for a burger when it's over.

BETSY: Sounds great. Listen—I really need to go. Gino's waiting for me.

BUBBA: Sure. Uh—see you tomorrow.

BETSY: Yeah. And good luck tonight! *(She exits.)*

BUBBA: Yo, Pop!

LUIGI *(enters from kitchen):* EY!

BUBBA: I'll wait for you in the car. *(He exits to outside.)*

LUIGI: Whatza matter for you, eh? *(He hangs up his apron, then walks toward exit. Then he stops and looks at the audience.)* Come on! Whatza matter for you, eh? My son, Lucia . . . *(pauses as he corrects himself)* Bubba. He's a gonna sing . . . *(pauses, looks up to heaven)* for his mama and me.

BUBBA *(enters from outside):* Yo, Pop! You are coming, aren't you?

LUIGI *(lovingly):* Whatza matter for you, eh? *(He puts arm around* BUBBA *and they exit.)*

THE END

PERFORMANCE LICENSING AGREEMENT

Lillenas Publishing Resources
Performance Licensing
P.O. Box 419527, Kansas City, MO 64141

Name _____

Organization _____

Address _____

City _____ State _____ ZIP _____

Play title __***MEET ME AT LUIGI'S***__ by Tom and Celesta Letchworth_____

Number of performances intended _____

Approximate dates _____

Amount remitted* $ _____

Mail to Lillenas at the address above.

Order performance copies of this script from your local bookstore or directly from the publisher (1-800-877-0700).

*$30.00 for the first performance; $20.00 for each subsequent performance. Payable in U.S. funds.